Craft Tequila:

WTF Does THAT Mean?

How to get past the marketing

and know a real craft tequila when you see one

By

M.A. "Mike" Morales

About The Author

M.A. "Mike" Morales is a tequila tastemaker and agave spirit influencer. His long-running spirits review show on www.TequilaAficionado.com, Sipping Off the Cuff, has run for over 1,000 episodes and counting, reviewing tequila, mezcal, sotol, raicilla, bacanora, and other Mexican spirits.

His experience and expertise in the agave spirits industry has made him a sought-after consultant, experienced journalist, and significant source for many national and international publications.

Mike has been a life-long bodybuilder and die-hard Dodgers fan, enjoys training table food, good cigars, fine living and traveling with his family, 4 cats and 3-legged dog.

Find Mike Morales Online

Personal Website

Tequila Aficionado

Facebook

Twitter

Instagram

Pinterest

LinkedIn

YouTube

Get invited to participate in Mike's upcoming Consumer Catador Course here.

To book a consultation with Mike Morales, visit his Facebook Page here.

Copyright

The Big Business of Kosher Tequila by
M.A. "Mike" Morales

Published by M.A. "Mike" Morales

www.TequilaSensei.com

www.TequilaAficionado.com

Coming Soon From Mike Morales

From Babes to Boss Ladies: Women in the Tequila and Mezcal Industries

I've had a special place in my heart for the unsung heroines and muses in tequila for a very long time. After reading Ilana Edelstein's The Patron Way, I felt it was time someone brought other women's stories to light – and what better place to do that than at the leader in tequila information since 1999 – *Tequila Aficionado*.

It all began with Tequila Boss Ladies and grew from there.

From Babes to Boss Ladies

The contributions of women who create some of the amazing spirits we enjoy, direct production and distillation, support educational efforts, own brands we love, and otherwise contribute to the tequila industry are often overlooked beyond the 90's throwback bikini-babe marketing efforts of brands. From Babes to Boss Ladies digs deep into the world of tequila and agave spirits and brings these ladies' stories to light.

Craft Tequila: WTF Does THAT Mean?

How to get past the marketing and know a real craft tequila when you see one

What does "Craft" mean for tequilas?

An interesting question crossed my desk concerning the term craft as it relates to tequila.

This person asked...

> *"The one thing I am finding is the definition of 'craft' is all over the place. What does craft mean to you? Do you think it is based on the*

*method, quantity, who makes it or
maybe all of these factors?"*

This reader went on to ask if I considered
a particular big name brand a craft tequila,
and if not, would I consider a certain
higher priced line from this same
transnational corporation that owns the
brand as a craft tequila.

Further, he confessed that two other well-
known brands could be considered "craft"
tequilas even though one of them had
reported sales of over 50,000 cases in
2013.

What does craft tequila mean to you?
Is it method, quantity, who makes it, or
maybe all of the above?

Craft by Definition

According to Merriam-Webster's online dictionary, my favorite definition is–

> *"...an activity that involves making something in a skillful way by using your hands."*

The word handcraft is defined as...

> *"...to make (something) by using your hands."*

There are even deeper meanings to craft as it relates to the beer, wine and spirits industries, but before I get to them, let me remind you of some tequila facts and a huge marketing myth.

Fact #1: *Tequila has its own geographic indication (GI). The blue weber agave from which it is made can only be grown, and tequila can only be produced, in specific states and regions in Mexico.*

Fact #2: *According to the Distilled Spirits Council of the United States (DISCUS), despite 13 million 9 liter cases of tequila sold in 2013, it is still–and always will remain–virtually last in sales volume behind whisk(e)y, gin, vodka and rum due to Fact #1.*

This brings me to the...

Tequila Marketing Myth–Borrowing Benefits

So, how does a PR or marketing firm with no real knowledge of what good or bad tequila is, convey the message that its client, usually a high powered, non-Mexican owned tequila brand (and all that that implies), is just as cool as the other kids who may or may not be as well funded?

Simple–

You "borrow" benefits from the guy ahead of you. You compare your tequila brand's features and benefits to the leader in the field, thus making your client "worthy by association."

From the moment that ***Herradura*** rested tequila in used ***Jack Daniels*** barrels to attract the American whiskey drinker decades ago, marketers have tried to disguise tequila (and mezcal, now, to some extent) as something else.

And because of Facts #1 and #2 above, tequila marketers have for years misled the public by borrowing benefits from wines, beers and all other spirits in a seeming effort to gain tequila's acceptance into the mainstream drinking public, and to increase sales.

Tequila marketers mislead the public by borrowing benefits from wines, beers and other spirits to sell more tequila.

Craft by Design

Here's what it means to produce a craft product in each of the following arenas.

The Brewers' Association defines craft as small ("6 million barrels of beer or less per year"), independent ("less than 25 percent of the craft brewery is owned or controlled by a beverage alcohol industry member that is not itself a craft brewer"), and traditional ("a brewer that has a majority of its total beverage alcohol volume in beers whose flavor derives from traditional or innovative brewing ingredients and their fermentation").

The American Craft Distillers Association's (ACDA) definition of craft gets trickier–

> *"...those whose annual production of distilled spirits from all sources does not exceed 750,000 proof gallons removed from bond (the amount on which excise taxes are paid.)"*

According to the **Alcohol and Tobacco Tax and Trade Bureau (TTB)**, a proof gallon needs an entire conversion table to figure out. We'll let you do the math, here.

The American Distilling Institute's (ADI) guidelines are similar but allow certified craft spirits a "maximum annual sales of 52,000 cases where the product is PHYSICALLY distilled and bottled on-site" and "maximum annual sales are less than 100,000 proof gallons."

Where wine is concerned, the **Department of Revenue** defines a "small winery" as any winery that produces less than 25,000 gallons of wine in a calendar year. A "farm winery," however, can produce up to 50,000 gallons of wine annually.

Some have even arbitrarily issued their own definition of small winery as one producing as little as 10,000 gallons per year, and a nano winery as generating only 500 gallons per year.

A simple Google search shows that each state has its own slightly different definition of what a craft wine or spirit is, and several states with popular wine growing regions like California, are constantly updating their definition to accommodate growing wineries.

The same growing concerns in the craft beer industry have prompted the **Brewer's Association** to update their ground rules to allow for larger craft producers.

The Revenge of Brewzilla

According to Impact Databank, a large chunk of the beer industry has surrendered significant market share (some 6.7 million barrels, or 93 million 2.25-gallon cases since 2009!) to the spirits industry. The only bright spot for the entire category is the resurgence of locally brewed craft or specialty beers increasing in volume by 14% to 20.2 million barrels.

These stats have not been lost on spirits marketers who follow trends in similar markets to practice borrowing benefits. The big brands like **_Miller-Coors, Anheuser Busch-Inbev (Budweiser)_** and others also have jumped onto the craft bandwagon by either investing in small breweries or by inferring in their marketing that they still make their beer by hand.

As **Ashley Routson**, a craft beer advocate famously known as **The Beer Wench**, and whose upcoming book **"The Beer Wench's Guide to Beer"** will be an unpretentious, comprehensive approach to beer, puts it...

> *"In my opinion, the fight over the word craft should be one of semantics, but instead, its become a battle of the egos."*

Routson goes on to say,

"The word 'craft' is not a synonym for the word 'good,' 'great' or 'better.' Many non-craft breweries and large tequila producers make world class beer and tequila—there is no argument there. You don't need to use the word craft to define your beverage as being good."

Beer journalist, **Mike Cortez**, whose pending book will be a part of the Beer Lovers series of books (**Beer Lover's Texas**), is also the co-founder of **The Texas Margarita Festival**, and feels that craft tequila should be held to the same strict standards as craft beer.

"We need to separate the garbage from the good stuff. [Like craft] beer that is only made with the basics, grain, water, hops and yeast, the brewers do not use additives or adjuncts to flavor the beer."

Cortez concludes,

"[Tequila] is a product that takes time, care and only the purest agave extraction. The distillers depend on the time to harvest the agave, baking the pinas and perfectly extracting the juices. Once it is distilled it is a product that is pure and only flavored by the barrel with no extra additives."

Tequila Industry consultant, **Chris Zarus**, innovator of **TequilaRack**, the world's first take home tequila tasting kit that deliberately includes samples of some of the finest small batch, micro-distilled reposado tequilas sourced from family run distilleries, takes the craft argument to a higher level.

> *"The word craft has unfortunately been abducted by the marketing department and now misleads the masses. We go to classes that advise us on how to make our brands 'craftier' with specialty releases with funny names [and] all owned by multinational conglomerates that work*

relentlessly to reduce costs via
cheaper ingredients and
mechanization."

Zarus believes that there are two industry definitions of craft which differ from what the consumer understands. They involve a specific recipe and a specific process.

Specific Recipe

In this craft version, the product is consistent and costs are contained.

> *"The Jim Koch's [founder of Samuel*
> *Adams beer] view that his recipe*
> *makes his beer craft regardless of*
> *the fact that MillerCoors brews it*

for the masses," explains Zarus. *"In [Koch's] opinion, its like a chef going to your house to cook his special recipe."*

"If you think about it in broad terms," reasons Zarus, *"all consumer products have a specific recipe. The difference here may be that the recipe is full flavored and is preferred by fewer due to its heartier taste."*

Specific Process

In this definition, the process is the craft.

Tequila Fortaleza, produced by famed fifth generation distiller, Guillermo Sauza, Zarus illustrates, *"[Is] very specific, old world, but not very mechanized. In this way the outcome varies by batch and the state of the local ingredients. The craft is the process."*

The downside, insists Zarus is that, *"...the product varies by batch, like some wines. There is a lack of product consistency. Some batches have more acclaim than others and the maker is not getting to charge the full price of the best batches."*

This last seeming liability has been turned into a profitable tequila marketing plan by some boutique brands like **Ocho** and **Charbay** who source their agave from single estates thus promoting the brand's terroir and creating buzz for individual vintages.

The Meaning and the Art Form

The two essential elements that Routson, Cortez and Zarus all agree upon are, first, that the craft process is the art form, whether in beer, wine or spirits.

The other factor that our panel of professionals agrees on is the battle of maintaining the true definition of the word craft.

We'll explore these issues and how you can define, select and measure a craft tequila next.

Blurred Lines

We've employed the use of more adjectives and descriptors to define, describe and distinguish one booze from another in the same category, as well as to give the illusion that it is actually closer to another booze in the leading categories.

Words like award-winning, artisanal, small-run, limited-production, hand-crafted, and boutique are reused over and over. So are micro-distilled, limited edition, small batch, small lot, organic (which we'll cover in-depth in a future book), single village, homespun, authentic, small-lot, prestige, signature, high end and reserve.

They all have real core meanings, but because we see them repeatedly in ads, billboards, packaging, shelf talkers and point of sale (POS) materials, the lines between meaning and true definitions get blurred.

For instance, the definition of the word premium as defined by the Distilled Spirits Council of the United States (DISCUS) is actually a pricing term. To the average consumer, however, it has come to mean quality. And when consumers' buying habits change and trade up, it has become known as premiumization.

There's no chance of spirits marketers discontinuing the use of the Tequila Marketing Myth of borrowing benefits any time soon.

How, then, do we really define and measure a craft tequila?

We'll show you how in a moment, but let's get two things straight right here–

Remember Fact #1? Tequila belongs in Mexico.

Though some American micro-distilleries have attempted to distill small batches of agave spirits, it has proven difficult and labor intensive due to it being produced from a plant that takes years to mature as opposed to grains, hops, and grapes that yield more frequent harvests.

It would be silly to define and measure craft tequila in ways that relate to wine, beer and other spirits created in the United States and abroad. There may be no boundaries in spirits marketing, but to impose limits on the number of barrels, bottles, and cases manufactured and sold by a tequila distillery in order to measure a craft product would have no jurisdiction whatsoever in Mexico.

Secondly–

There Is No Backpedaling

The Beer Wench, Ashley Routson said it best when interviewed for this article:

> "No one wants to fault the big guys for being successful–that is not what this argument is about. My main question is–how big is too big? And as long as a company stays independently-owned, does that mean it will always be craft?"

Indeed, both the craft beer and spirits segments are growing at such a fast rate, that the Brewer's Association has changed its definition multiple times. This has allowed the burgeoning brewers more room to expand. And as spirits writer, **Wayne Curtis**, discusses in his article from **The Atlantic**, the alarming growth rate of small distilleries is having an effect on the quality of the finished craft product due to a shortage of experienced distillers.

As a consequence of this exponential growth, in both the craft beer and craft spirits categories, the process–the art form itself–is getting watered down.

Rant Alert!

Let's face it–

No one gets into the tequila business to be a failure. Everyone wants to be on top. And once you get there, the challenge is to stay on top.

We know how arduous the tequila hero's journey is.

No one with a business plan ever said, "I'm going to mass produce my lousy tequila and once I've flooded the shelves with my swill and lost market share, I'm going to distill a tequila the old fashioned way."

Don't pretend to continue to still make your tequila like you have over the past 250 years, either!

You are not that home based family operation still harvesting agaves by mule and macerating piñas with a tahona, any more.
That family's history was forgotten when the brand was sold.

And just because you build a separate, smaller facility on your distillery property to produce a more labor intensive line (and even petition to do so under another NOM number!) when you have never attempted to do so in the first place, does not make your more expensive line a craft tequila.

Build a token distillery, get a fresh nom number and call it craft? Rubbish!

Moreover, just because you happen to be a colossal consumer of agave, still being emulated for your unique style of 1980's spirits marketing, and prefer to see things differently, don't expect the rest of us to swallow your slant.

> *Don't market tequila like you did 20 years ago. We won't believe you.*

The Craft Tequila Gauntlet

Following are some tips and suggestions that may help guide you in making more informed decisions when selecting, defining and measuring a craft tequila.

#1: NOM list

By Mexican law, every tequila must display a number that corresponds to the legal representative, tequila producer or distillery in which it was produced. Tracing that number to the CRT's list of distilleries, you can discover what other brands are manufactured under that specific number, and presumably, in that specific factory.

Logic dictates that the fewer labels a fabrica (factory) produces means more care should be taken with its one or two flagship brands.

Logic also dictates the opposite when you see many different brands appearing under a particular NOM number.

Whether the distillery produces only a few lines, or many contract brands for others, is not necessarily a sign of the tequila's craftiness or quality, but it's a start.

[You can view and download the most recent NOM lists from our website here.](#)

#2: Pedigree

Taking a pointer from panel expert, Chriz Zarus' now industry classic article, "Change is at Hand for the Tequila Market, Part II," a craft brand with a good chance of survival in the market will be one that *"You, your distillery, and your brand have generations of lineage."*

Meet-the-Maker dinner pairings, industry meetings and on-premise tastings showcasing a craft tequila will more than likely feature the brand owner or the master distiller behind the brand.

In some cases, a well respected Brand Ambassador (not the gal or guy with the tight t-shirt!) will stand in for the owner if there is a scheduling conflict.

Again, this is not a guarantee of craftiness or quality, but most family owned brands will stand behind (or in front) of their tequila with pride.

#3: Distillery ownership/partnership/co-op

Another tip from Zarus' treatise that could be useful in determining whether a craft tequila will be successful or not is, *"Your company does...own at least a portion of the distillery that produces your product."*

This was successfully accomplished by the owners of **Suerte Tequila**, one of the few still produced with a tahona (milling stone). In order to ensure the quality of their tequila and to regulate the brand's eventual growth, **Lance Sokol** and **Laurence Spiewak** purchased the distillery.

Does your craft tequila have some skin in the game? Most good ones do and will proudly make that information public.

#4: Agave and land ownership

Similar to #3 above, some craft brands are owned by families with ties to the land and own their own agave. In some instances, they may or may not own all or a portion of the distillery where they produce their tequila.

In the midst of this current agave shortage, this one asset could make or break a craft brand. This information should be readily available in POS material, but is also not a guarantee of quality or craftiness.

#5: Use of a Diffuser

While considered a legitimate tool in tequila production efficiency and has the full blessing of the CRT, the use of a diffuser is a dead giveaway that shortcuts are being taken.

As noted agave ethno-botanist, **Ana Valenzuela** so succinctly declared in this open letter...

> *"...prohibir el uso de difusores (hidrólisis de jugos de agave) que les quita "el alma" (el sabor a agave cocido) a nuestros destilados, únicos en el mundo por su*

complejidad aromatic y de
sabores.”

["...to prohibit the use of diffusers
(in hydrolysis of agave juices) that
takes the "soul" (the flavor of baked
agave) out of our native distillates,
singular in the world for its
complexities of aromas and
flavors."]

Can a diffuser tequila be considered a
craft tequila?
This is also in keeping with Zarus'
definition of preserving the process as the
art form or craft outlined earlier.

Using a diffuser is a closely guarded
secret by most mid-sized to large

distilleries and hard to spot. You can read more about them here.

#6: Organic

If there are any products that deserve to be described with the aforementioned adjectives that spirits marketers are freely throwing around these days to denote a handcrafted tequila, mezcal, or other agave distillate, they are in the organic segment.

Stringent regulations are required in both farm to distillery, and then from factory to bottle, to be given the designation organic and the permission to use the *USDA* seal that appears prominently on the labels.

By virtue of being organic, the process is considered much more natural and is inherently small batched.

Can we automatically consider organic tequila "craft" tequila?

But, not every brand has the budget to become a certified organic tequila. In addition, some brands may simply not see the value of being certified as organic, especially since some organic certifying agencies have been looked upon with mistrust in recent years.

Still, it could arguably be the most reliable indicator of a craft agave distillate.

#7: Transparency

This might be the toughest test of all.

As we mentioned above, many brands prefer to play their cards close to the vest. By the same token, many family owned brands are fiercely proud of their origins and will gladly tell you the truth, the whole truth, and nothing but the truth.

> *Is your craft tequila brand willing to tell you their story, or just tell you a story?*

Many of the more popular craft tequila brands are helmed by creators who are delightfully flamboyant and outspoken, as well.

Craft by Any Other Name

As our reader stated, the meaning of craft is "all over the place" and then some.

With mixology being the leading trend driving the spirits industry and demand for better ingredients on the rise, this means quality tequila is essential for those creating crafted cocktails (there's that word again!).

But, with the invention of the wildly popular *Michelada* cocktail, a margarita (which is the favorite way Americans consume tequila) served with a beer bottle upside down in a margarita glass, and chilled tequila on tap, there will surely be more cross pollination between adult beverage categories.

We've already seen this with tequila brands selling their used aging barrels to small brewers to create signature craft beers, as well as tequila aged in barrels bought from other brand named spirits.

This will only lead to even more crossovers between categories caused by inspired spirits marketers, PR firms, uninformed spirits journalists and bloggers, and multinational corporations.

Borrowing benefits has been the norm for some time.

There will always be those who deliberately hide the truth or feed false information to the media and practice opacity. We can't control what they will say and do.

The key is to become educated and informed about a tequila's recipe and process. Using the *Craft Tequila Gauntlet* above can certainly help in making the right choices.

The Top 20 Craft Tequilas You've Overlooked

In early August of 2016, I received an email from **USA Today** asking me to weigh in on their craft spirits-themed Readers' Choice contests, and in our case (at press time), the soon-to-be-launched craft tequilas list.

I'll be honest, I dread these lists. What's worse is, I dread being asked to participate in compiling them.

Let me tell you why.

It's A List

In the Digital Age, everyone wants things in bite sized form and they want it now. It is also proven that numbered lists draw attention.

And, there are so many of them out there on the Interwebs–

Fifty Ways to Leave Your Lover...

The 10 Best Ways to Cheat On Your Mate...

Six Ways Your Cat Plots to Kill You...

A Word About Your Sins

Ever wonder why those numbered titles are so enticing?
It's because they are aimed at the 7 Deadly Sins.

A steadfast rule of copywriters is to compose content that elicits an emotional response from readers to take action.
To drive your particular sin even further to cause you to read the content, the word YOU is hammered into every title.

> *[Editor's note: See what I did with my title? You choose which sin fits best for YOU.]*

Craft Is A Buzzword

As we thoroughly examined previously, term *craft* has been kidnapped by marketers writing fancy copy to confuse the consumer.

Only 10?

While the instructions in the email required at least 20 selections from me, the contest will butcher the selections down to only 10–

Selected by those who are unaware of what a craft tequila really is, and...

Curated by someone whose job it is to find ways to engage USA Today's readers.

It's A Contest

When our COO, Lisa Pietsch, examined the contest website and the myriad of other pre-existing lists, she found that this is a clever way for USA Today to increase reader engagement.

Reader engagement translates to readers' time spent on USA Today's mammoth website, which in turn translates to money they charge advertisers.

The term we use is "sticky" as in spider's web sticky.

Which leads me to–

Paid Advertisers

Having been paid to ghost write Editor's Choice lists in the past, I am fully aware that many times, spirits sponsors of major magazines and websites tend to sneak onto them.

This, despite my vehement objections to the editors that such a move invalidates the list altogether.

So, before any of the Usual Suspects wind up on USA Today's 10 Best Readers' Choice Awards Craft Tequilas list, here are my selections.

Bear in mind, I was limited to only twenty brands.

The Top 20 Craft Tequilas You've Overlooked

In no particular order…

1. Fortaleza
2. T1 Tequila Uno
3. Tears of Llorona
4. Suerte
5. Siembra Azul
6. Siembra Valles
7. Tapatio
8. Tequila G4
9. ArteNOM 1414
10. ArteNOM 1580
11. ArteNOM 1146
12. ArteNOM 1549

The Fallout

Whether any of my selections make the cut, remains to be seen.

Depending on who the other *"tequila experts"* were that contributed to the final list to be voted on, the results, if nothing else, should be interesting.

One thing is for certain–
Not everyone will be happy.

USA Today's List as Released

T1 Tequila Uno Wins Best Craft Tequila Brand!

Embajador Tequila, Suerte Tequila, DesMaDre Tequila and Tequila G4 also winners

In order to be called tequila, this spirit distilled from the juices blue agave must be made in specific regions of Mexico, most prominently Jalisco and the town of tequila. While no tequilas are produced in the United States, we wanted to find the best craft tequila brands available in the country, and to do so, we asked a pair of tequila experts to nominate their favorites for our readers to vote on.

Unlike other spirits, tequila brands often share distilleries – there are about 70 of them producing more than 500 brands – so it's often the brand rather than the distillery that indicates quality. Many of these 10 winners for best craft tequila brand use traditional methods. Many of the brand owners grow their own agave and personally oversee the entire *tequila-making process. All produce high-quality, distinctive tequilas available in the U.S. market.*

The top 10 winners in the category Best Craft Tequila Brand are as follows:

1. *T1 Tequila Uno*
2. *Embajador Tequila*
3. *Suerte Tequila*
4. *DesMaDre Tequila*
5. *Tequila G4*
6. *Tequila Gran Dovejo*
7. *Siete Leguas*
8. *Tequila Tapatío*
9. *Dulce Vida Tequila*
10. *Tequila Don Modesto*

A panel of experts partnered with 10Best editors to picked the initial 20 nominees, and the top 10 winners were determined by popular vote. Experts M.A. "Mike" Morales (TequilaAficionado.com) and Grover Sanschagrin (TasteTequila.com) were chosen based on their expertise in the craft tequila industry.

Other nominated brands included Casa Noble Tequila, Don Fulano, IXÁ Organic Tequila, Pasote Tequila, Siembra Spirits, Tears of Llorona, Tequila Alquimia, Tequila ArteNOM, Tequila Fortaleza and Tequila Ocho.

Congratulations to all our winning brands!

20 Reasons Why USA Today's Craft Tequilas List Failed

Let's Review...

Previously, I enumerated my reasons for dreading my participation in USA Today's 10 Best Craft Tequila list.

In my experience, something inevitably goes awry with these sorts of "listicles," and it usually starts with the editor.

Contrary to the galloping propaganda disseminated by some press releases, there were *no* additional USA Today Editors involved in accumulating the original list of twenty craft tequilas. Only the two recruited "experts" were involved.

This time around, I blame the *curator* of these lists whose job it is to engage USA Today's readership, which in turn leads to its increased ad revenue.

Now that the excitement has died down, it's time to assess the damage done by deliberately withheld facts, and to clear the air of unbridled misinformation.

The Top 20 Reasons Why USA Today's Top 10 Craft Tequila List Sucks

[Caution: Rants Ahead]

1. Lack of Respect.

When someone asks you to accrue a list on your area of expertise, you, as the curator, must assume that that person takes this task very seriously, especially since you've taken the time to background check the expert who is going to help you get *PAID*.

2. Lack of Communication.

When this expert communicates questions to you via email or phone, be aware that this person expects a timely answer, especially when *YOU* have asked him for his list by a certain deadline.

3. Lack of Trust.

When you deliberately avoid answering questions about who else is involved in accruing a list for you, you immediately raise suspicion.

As with most "industry experts," we tend to know one another. In this instance, we could have worked in tandem to come up with a more complete list for the benefit of serious consumers.

4. Lack of Respect for Relationships.

You must also assume that the expert not only admires those items on his list, but personally knows each producer of those items and has forged lasting relationships with them over the years.

5. More Lack of Respect for Relationships.

Because of these relationships, you must assume the expert is also highly regarded by those craft producers that he has included on his list.

6. Lack of Understanding the **Craft** Segment.

By virtue of being **craft distillers**, you must understand that they are *not* made of money like the Big Boys. These guys literally live by their shoestrings.

7. Lack of Transparency.

Total and complete transparency when communicating with your experts is vital. Explaining what opportunities and hidden fees await the winners is of utmost importance as that intelligence could alter the final list.

8. Lack of Vergüenza (shame).

Where the *HELL* do you get off asking the winners for money for the licensing rights to use your seals, medals and trophies?

9. Lack of Seriousness.

Do you realize that you are asking for similar fees by more respected and reputable spirits judging contests like the San Francisco World Spirits Competition or the SIP Awards?

10.   Lack of Consideration.

Do you see that this lack of transparency on your part on behalf of USA Today could possibly put the expert's friendships and reputation at risk?

11. Lack of Realistic Expectations.

Do you really believe that these craft brands will fork over money for a meaningless popularity contest– for *bragging* rights?

12. Underestimating the Brands.

How stupid do you think they (or we, the judges) are?

13. Concealment of True Intentions.

Do you get that we understand that these contests you curate for USA Today are only to generate reader engagement which in turn determines your pricing to advertisers?

14.   Greediness.

Double dip, much?

15.   Conscious Collateral Damage.

Do you catch on that the winning and losing brands on this list probably now believe that the experts knew about the additional costs to the winners but chose not to divulge this information to them?

16.   Lack of Good Faith.

Most all professionally held beer, wine, and spirits competitions openly inform participants of additional licensing costs to the winners. USA Today deliberately chose to keep this information from their experts.

17.   Elimination Due to Perceived Lack of Relevance.

Was it fair for you to eliminate those craft tequila brands because they had little or no social media presence?

18.   Lack of Foresight on Your Part.

Bet you didn't see that one coming, huh?

19.   Naïveté On My Part.

I only reluctantly became involved to help promote these deserving craft tequila brands. *(Unpaid by USA Today and unpaid by any brands.)*

20.   Underhandedness.

Thanks for cheapening the craft tequila segment, USA Today.

Tequila Marketing Happy Talk

Some well-meaning follower posted on our Facebook page this answer to a press release referring to <u>Espolón</u> Tequila...

"PSA: "super premium" has no real meaning—it's marketing happy talk." While we're inclined to believe that sneaky marketers have hijacked the word *premium* and turned it into a buzzword, in all actuality, it is a spirits pricing term.

Let's Review

As we pointed out earlier, DISCUS, the national trade association and lobbyist representing the leading producers and marketers of distilled spirits in the United

States, separates all booze into four
categories–
*Value, Premium, High End Premium,
and Super Premium.*

**[Note the absence of the
term, Ultra Premium.]**

The confusion stems from the fact that
DISCUS lists the price points of each
particular spirit by supplier revenue per
case, not by retail price per bottle.

It is DISCUS' industry-focused terms that
are the culprit, and marketers have
indelibly embedded *premium* into
consumer's minds like an embarrassing
tattoo on a mixologist's forearm.

Think Like a Marketer

[Warning: You might want to shower after this segment.]

Webster's Online Dictionary defines **premium** as *"a price that is higher than the regular price."*

Want to think like a marketer?

Then, run *premium* through Webster's Thesaurus and inhale deeply as if you've just stumbled upon a secret cava filled to the ceiling with barrels of resting añejos.

Revel in the treasure trove of descriptors like Robert Duvall in Apocalypse Now.

A Stroll Down the Tequila Aisle

Now that you've toweled off, take a look at DISCUS' 2015 Industry Review Supplemental Tables, here.
Scroll to the section titled *Distilled Spirits Pricing Categories* and notice the names listed under *Major Brands,* especially those in the Tequila segment.

Bear in mind that all spirits categories are measured by how well or badly the Big Boys are performing. Your preferred craft label may not even be mentioned.

Now, pretend you're in the Tequila Aisle of your favorite liquor store and ask yourself—

Would I buy this tequila?

Whether your answer is yes or no, determine where your preferred tequila brand is priced and pigeonholed.

Value, Premium, High End Premium and Super Premium.

Are they within a few bucks of the Usual Suspects, or are they completely out of your ballpark?

By the way, if you're drinking at the Ultra Premium range, I have swamp land in

Arizona that I'd like to unload, er, sell to you.

Falling For Marketing Happy Talk

Next, just for kicks and giggles, take a gander at DISCUS' US Tequila Market at a Glance, here.

Look closely at the astronomical growth of the High End Premium and Super Premium divisions since 2002-2003. This trend even has a name–

"Premiumisation"

How's that for a buzzword?

Depending on which categories your favorite tequilas land, are you comfortable paying those prices?

Put another way–

Are you happy for supporting the Big Boys all these years?

Remember, there is no shame in sipping value tequilas. We won't judge you. When in doubt, turn to our <u>tequila reviews</u> to help with your buying decisions.

Go ahead...

Reach for that box of tissues, pour yourself a **craft** tequila, and vow never again to fall for the marketing happy talk.

More By M.A. "Mike" Morales

Vinazas: The Tequila Industry's Dirty Little Secret

A Responsible Consumer's Guide to Finding the Best Tequilas to Purchase and Drink

From August 2 to August 6, 2008, I was invited to join small batch distiller, David Suro of tequila Siembra Azúl, and a host of other educators and key people studying the cultural, anthropological, historical, and ecological aspects of the tequila industry in the beautiful Highlands of Jalisco, Mexico.

We would concentrate on touring distilleries specifically in Arandas and Atotonilco. David's plan was to gather these brilliant minds together in one place and videotape a round table discussion of the issues currently affecting the Los Altos region.

Among the participants was Doctor of Anthropolgy, José de Jesús Hernández López (Pepe to his friends) from the Centro Universitario de Los Altos. He would be, and still is, my guide for this investigation.

Is your favorite brand of tequila eco-friendly, or are you directly contributing to the uncontrolled watershed pollution of the Paisaje Agavero by supporting your brand's total disregard for the environment?

The time has come to not only drink responsibly, but to also think responsibly and purchase accordingly. This book is here to help you do just that - become a better informed consumer of agave spirits.

[Buy Now at Amazon](#)

The Big Business of Kosher Tequila

Not all tequilas are created equal.
An urgent text message about Kosher tequilas from an agave beverage manager

at a thriving new bar in New York City, and the resulting questions raised from research into this misunderstood market from all points--tequila and mezcal brand owners, consumers, and rabbinical representatives of the Jewish faith--prompted me to finally discuss the positive, often flawed, and vastly under served kosher tequila and mezcal segments of the market.

__Buy Now at Amazon__